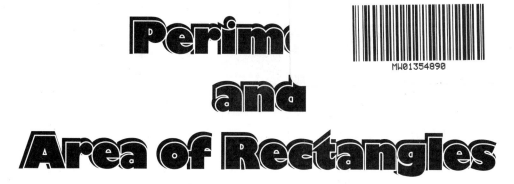

Perimeter and Area of Rectangles

Developed and Published
by
AIMS Education Foundation

This book contains materials developed by the AIMS Education Foundation. **AIMS** (**A**ctivities **I**ntegrating **M**athematics and **S**cience) began in 1981 with a grant from the National Science Foundation. The non-profit AIMS Education Foundation publishes hands-on instructional materials that build conceptual understanding. The foundation also sponsors a national program of professional development through which educators may gain expertise in teaching math and science.

Copyright © 2010 by the AIMS Education Foundation

All rights reserved. No part of this book or compact disc may be reproduced or transmitted in any form or by any means—graphic, electronic, or mechanical, including photocopying, taping, or information storage/retrieval systems—except as noted below.

- A person or school purchasing this AIMS publication is hereby granted permission to make up to 200 copies of any portion of it, provided these copies will be used for educational purposes and only at that school site. The accompanying compact disc contains all the printable pages for the publication. No files on the compact disc may be shared or altered by any means.

  Adobe® Acrobat® Reader (version 5.0 or higher) is required to access files on the compact disc. Adobe® Acrobat® Reader can be downloaded at no charge at adobe.com.

- An educator providing a professional-development workshop is granted permission to make enough copies of student activity sheets to use the lessons one time with one group.

AIMS users may purchase unlimited duplication rights for making additional copies or for use at more than one school site. Contact Duplication Rights.

AIMS Education Foundation
P.O. Box 8120, Fresno, CA 93747-8120 • 888.733.2467 • aimsedu.org

ISBN 978-1-60519-029-7

Printed in the United States of America

Welcome to the AIMS Essential Math Series!

Essential Math uses real-world investigations, comics, and animation to engage students and help them discover and make sense of key mathematical concepts.

The units in this series are narrowly focused, conceptually developed, and carefully sequenced to provide a continuum of introduction, development, and reinforcement of the essential ideas.

A typical *Essential Math* unit includes five components:

Investigations form the heart of each lesson. Through guided hands-on exploration, students discover and make sense of the essential ideas.

Comics provide a model of effective instruction and make the content knowledge explicit. Students can use them to review learning or clarify experiences from the investigations. They also provide reading within the content area.

Animation and Video dynamically and visually summarize the essential concepts. They facilitate a deeper understanding and provide a powerful and meaningful memory.

Problem Solving activities help students apply and reinforce the concepts in unique ways.

Assessments provide an opportunity for students to apply their learning and for teachers to determine what depth of understanding has been gained.

The accompanying CD includes the comics and animations, as well as the student pages in pdf to facilitate printing and use on interactive boards. It may also include video help for activities as appropriate.

The comics and animations are also on our website (www.aimsedu.org) in case you want students to preview or review them as homework. The book contains a reduced-page version of the comics. The CD has both full-page and reduced-page versions so you can use the ones that best suit your needs.

Whether you use this unit in your regular classroom, for intervention, or as the basis for a summer school or after-school program, it will provide a rich and meaningful learning experience for your students.

Perimeter and Area of Rectangles
Table of Contents

Welcome to the AIMS Essential Math Series!

BIG IDEA: Perimeter is the distance around a shape. For a rectangle, the perimeter is the sum of the lengths of its four sides.

Lesson One: What is the Distance Around the Object?

Day 1

Investigation *What is the Distance Around the Object?* 7

To develop a concept of perimeter as a measure of the distance around, string is wrapped around different objects and compared.

Comics *Measuring Distance Around* 8

Reviews the concept of perimeter and defines it from the meaning of its origin.

Lesson Two: Picturing Perimeter

Day 2

Investigation *Picturing Perimeter* 9

Cutting straws to form polygons and measuring the combined lengths of the straws develops the concept of perimeter as the sum of the lengths of the sides of a polygon.

Comics *Picturing Perimeter* 12

Reviews or clarifies the concept of perimeter as a sum of the lengths of the sides of a polygon.

Lesson Three: Side Line Counts

Day 3

Investigation *Side Line Counts* 13

Measuring perimeters by counting unit lengths on polygons establishes the concept of number as related to length.

Lesson Four: Side Talk About Rectangles

Day 4

Investigation Side Talk About Rectangles 17

By forming rectangles with strips of paper, the concept of a rectangle having two pairs of congruent sides is used to find the perimeter of rectangles.

Animation Some Walk Abouts 20

The perimeter of a rectangle is solved in three ways to develop multiple strategies to determine the perimeter of a rectangle.

Comics Side Talk About Rectangles 21

Explores multiple ways to find the perimeter of rectangles from a conceptual level.

Day 5

Problem Solving Perimeter Stories 23

Students encounter meaningful applications for finding the perimeters of rectangles.

BIG IDEA: Area is a measure of covering and is measured in squares units. The area of a rectangle is determined by multiplying the number of squares in a row by the number of rows in the rectangle.

Lesson Five: Measuring Puzzle Pieces

Day 6

Investigation Measuring Puzzle Pieces 25

Establishes area as a measuring of covering with square units. Also develops the concept of combining areas to get total area.

Comics Measuring Puzzle Pieces 29

Uses the context of puzzle pieces to develop the concept of area as a covering with square units.

Lesson Six: Rainbow Rectangles

Day 7

Investigation Rainbow Rectangles 31

Develops the idea of finding area of a rectangle by multiplying the number of squares in a row by the number of rows.

Comics Rainbow Rectangles 35

Begins the development of a formula or process of measuring area of a rectangle by relating it to the number of squares in a row and the number of rows in the rectangle.

PERIMETER AND AREA OF RECTANGLES © 2010 AIMS Education Foundation

Lesson Seven: Covering Patterns

Day 8

Investigation *Covering Patterns* 37

Reinforces the process of multiplying the number of squares in a row by the number of rows in the rectangle.

Comics *Covering Patterns* 41

Reinforces the concept of finding area by multiplying the number of squares in a row by the number of rows in a rectangle.

Practice 42

Students will apply what they have learned to irregular polygons.

Lesson Eight: Framing the Facts

Day 9

Investigation *Framing the Facts* 43

Tracing rectangles and recording their areas develops the multiplication table. This relates area to multiplication as the dimensions of a rectangle are seen as factors and the area of the rectangle is the product.

Animation *Framing the Facts* 45

The multiplication table is developed dynamically with multiple rectangles. This provides an opportunity to practice area measurement and the multiplication facts.

Comics *Framing the Facts* 46

Develops the relationship between area and the multiplication table to reinforce the concept of area as a multiplicative process.

Day 10

Problem Solving *Square Thinking About Party Trays* 47

Students apply and practice determining perimeter and area in the context of building party trays covered with brownies.

Comics *Square Thinking About Party Trays* 50

Covers the problem-solving process that might arise when dealing with an application of area and perimeter in a problem-solving situation.

Day 11

Assessment *Perimeter and Area of Rectangles* 53

Two situations, one holding perimeter constant, the other with area constant, allow for multiple practice and assessment of understanding.

Glossary 57
National Standards and Materials 58
The Story of Perimeter and Area of Rectangles 59
Using Comics to Teach Math 61
Using Animations to Teach Math 62
The AIMS Model of Learning 63

What is the Distance Around an Object?

The purpose of this beginning investigation is to focus on the idea of **distance around**. After measuring the distance around a number of objects found in the classroom, students will be introduced to the word *perimeter*, which means *measure around*.

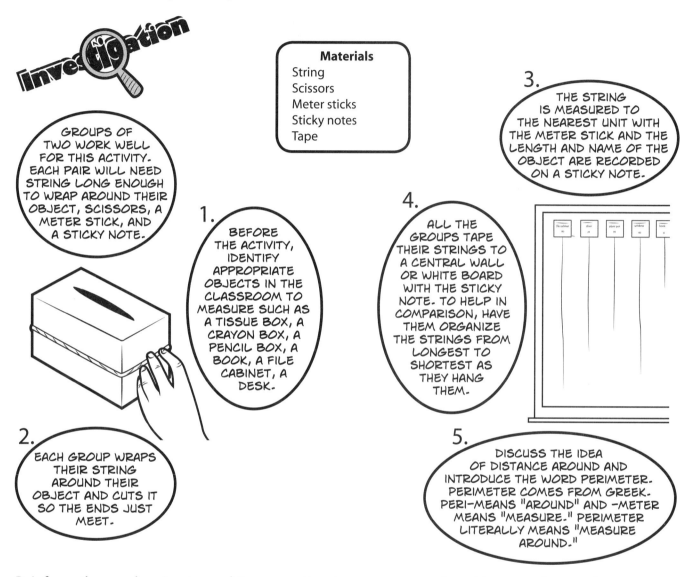

Reinforce the word perimeter and its connection to measurement by asking questions such as:
- What object had the longest perimeter?
- What object had the shortest perimeter?
- What is the difference between the longest and shortest perimeter?
- How much longer was your object's perimeter than the shortest perimeter?
- How much shorter was your object's perimeter than the longest perimeter?
- What is the combined length of the longest and shortest perimeter?

The comic reviews the concept of perimeter and defines it from the meaning of its origin.

PICTURING PERIMETER

The focus of this lesson is on the meaning of perimeter (distance around). Perimeters are linear and are about adding lengths of the sides that make up a shape. The act of matching straws to the sides of a figure drawn on paper and then laying out the straws to form one line helps students picture the idea that perimeter is the length around the shape.

Investigation

Materials
Straws or coffee stirrers
Scissors

GROUPS OF TWO WORK WELL FOR THIS ACTIVITY. EACH PAIR WILL NEED SIX STRAWS AND SCISSORS.

MOST STUDENTS WILL FIND THE SUM OF THE EDGES. IF MORE EXPERIENCE IS NEEDED, THE CUT STRAWS CAN BE LAID AROUND THE FIGURES.

TO AVOID THE NEED FOR SCISSORS, YOU MAY CHOOSE TO CUT THE STRAWS TO LENGTH BEFORE THE LESSON. EACH GROUP WILL NEED TWO STRAWS OF EACH LENGTH OF FOUR, FIVE, SIX, AND SEVEN CENTIMETERS.

MEASURE AND RECORD EACH SEGMENT SEPARATELY.

STRAWS OF THE CORRECT LENGTH MAY BE USED SEVERAL TIMES WHEN MEASURING THE FOUR FIGURES.

THE STRAWS ARE CUT TO THE LENGTH OF EACH SIDE OF THE FIGURES AND LAID AROUND THE PERIMETER OF ONE FIGURE AT A TIME.

LAYING THE STRAWS IN A LINE ON THE RULER MEASURES THE PERIMETER OF THE FIGURE TO THE CLOSEST CENTIMETER.

HAVE STUDENTS LAY OUT THE STRAWS TO FORM A SHAPE. THE SHAPE IS DRAWN BY TRACING THE EDGE OF EACH STRAW.

HAVE THE STUDENTS EXCHANGE THEIR FIGURES TO CONCUR.

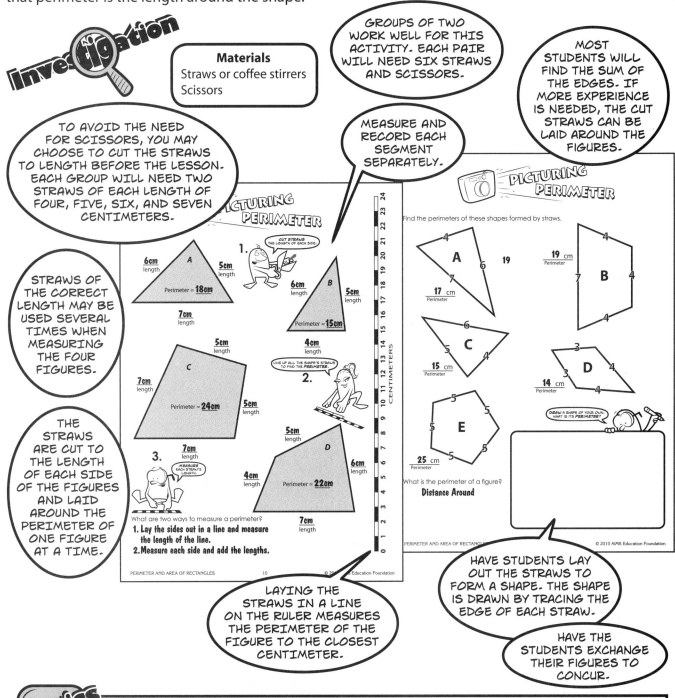

Comics

Reviews or clarifies the concept of perimeter as a sum of the lengths of the sides of a polygon.

PERIMETER AND AREA OF RECTANGLES © 2010 AIMS Education Foundation

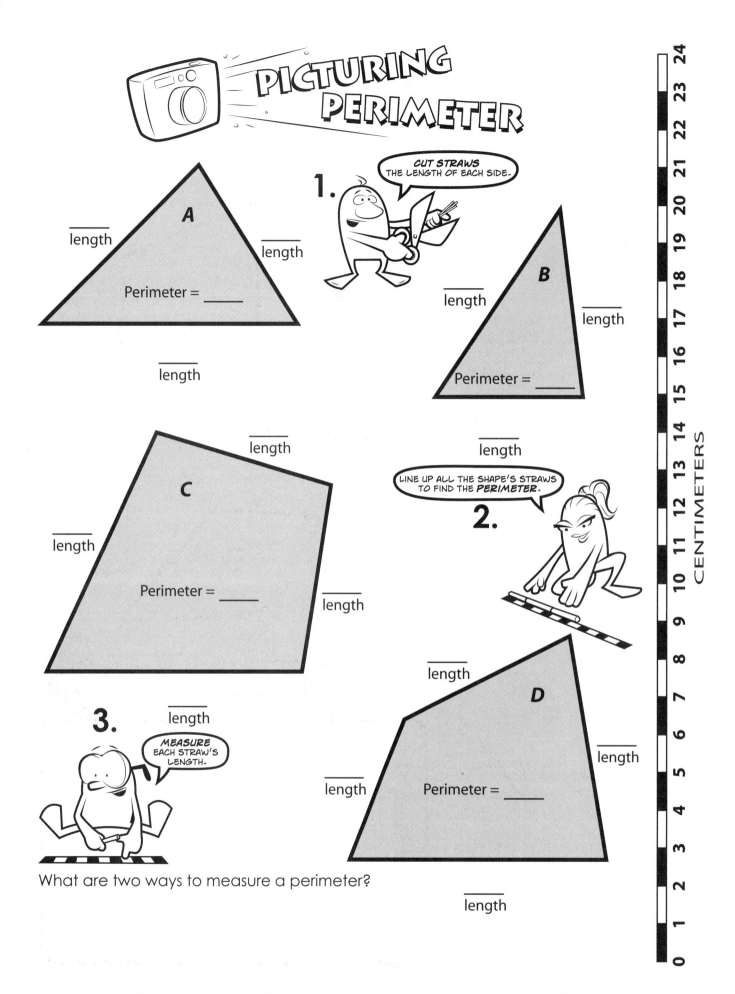

PICTURING PERIMETER

Find the perimeters of these shapes formed by straws.

A: sides 4, 6, 7
_____ cm
Perimeter

B: sides 4, 4, 4, 7
_____ cm
Perimeter

C: sides 6, 5, 4
_____ cm
Perimeter

D: sides 3, 3, 4, 4
_____ cm
Perimeter

E: sides 5, 5, 5, 5, 5
_____ cm
Perimeter

What is the perimeter of a figure?

DRAW A SHAPE OF YOUR OWN. WHAT IS ITS PERIMETER?

PERIMETER AND AREA OF RECTANGLES   11   © 2010 AIMS Education Foundation

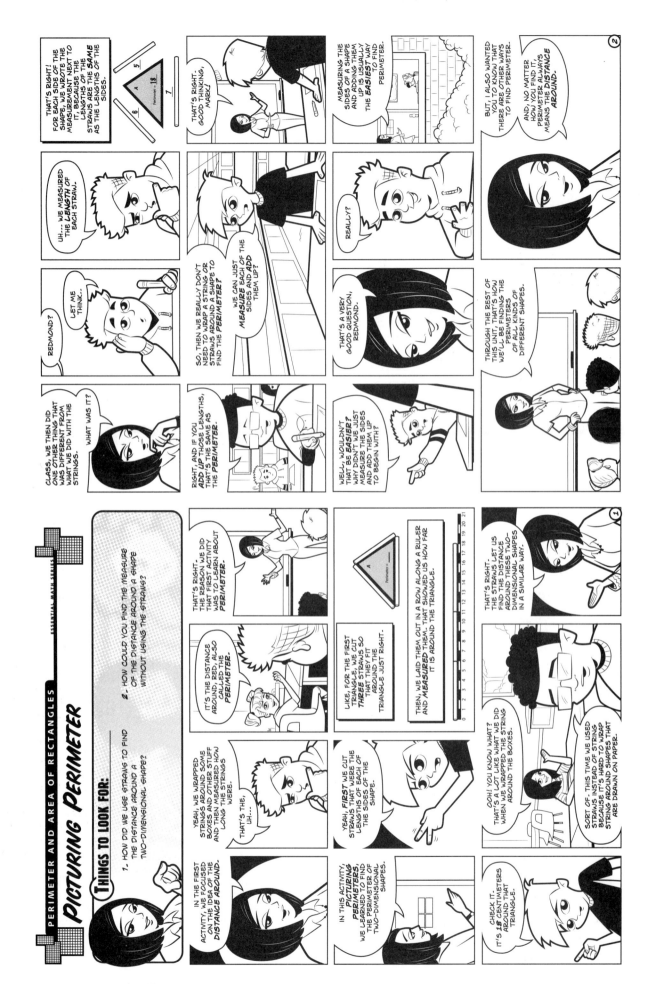

Side Line Counts

The focus of this lesson is to find the perimeter of different shapes by counting the unit lengths around the shape. Using the edge of a unit square to mark the units of length emphasizes perimeter as a one-dimensional measure.

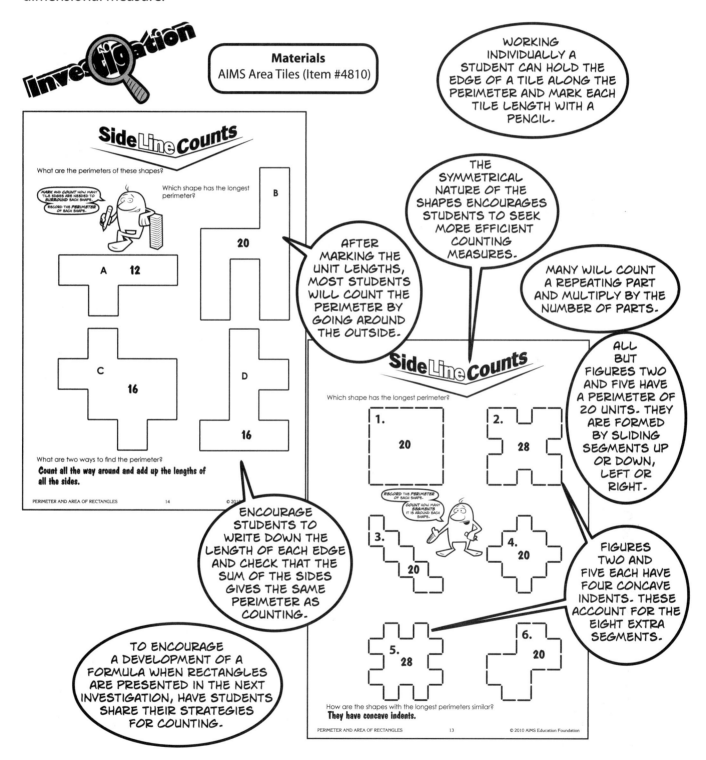

Side Line Counts

What are the perimeters of these shapes?

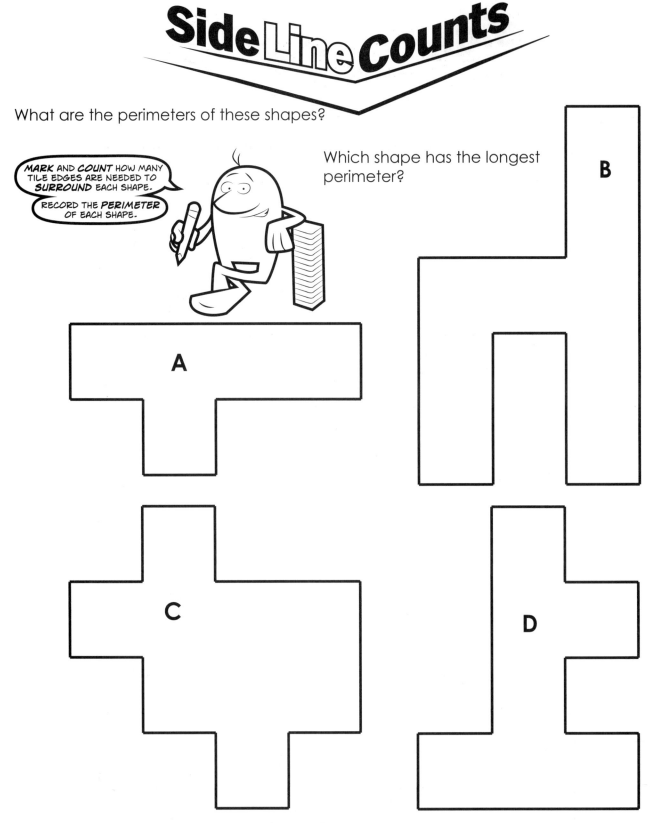

What are two ways to find the perimeter?

PERIMETER AND AREA OF RECTANGLES

Side Line Counts

Which shape has the longest perimeter?

How are the shapes with the longest perimeters similar?

SIDE TALK ABOUT RECTANGLES

What are some different ways to find the perimeter of a measured rectangle?

By constructing a variety of rectangles, students discover different ways to find the perimeter. Adding the lengths of the sides, adding the lengths of two adjacent sides and doubling the sum, or doubling the length and the width and summing the products are three ways.

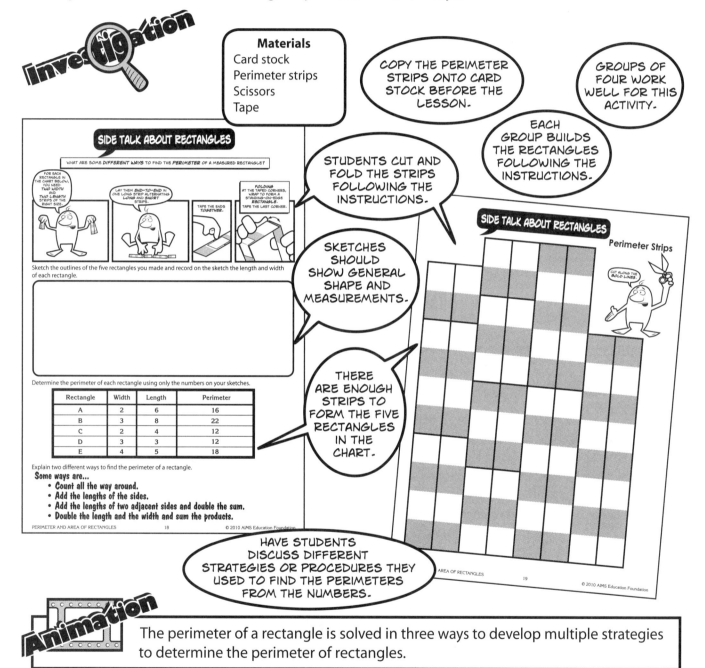

Animation: The perimeter of a rectangle is solved in three ways to develop multiple strategies to determine the perimeter of rectangles.

Comics: The comic explores multiple ways to find the perimeter of rectangles from a conceptual level.

Sketch the outlines of the five rectangles you made and record on the sketch the length and width of each rectangle.

Determine the perimeter of each rectangle using only the numbers on your sketches.

Rectangle	Width	Length	Perimeter
A	2	6	
B	3	8	
C	2	4	
D	3	3	
E	4	5	

Explain two different ways to find the perimeter of a rectangle.

PERIMETER AND AREA OF RECTANGLES

SIDE TALK ABOUT RECTANGLES

Perimeter Strips

Cut along the bold lines.

PERIMETER AND AREA OF RECTANGLES

SIDE TALK ABOUT RECTANGLES

Some Walk Abouts

How can you determine the perimeter of a rectangle?

How did the feet walk to measure the perimeter of this rectangle?

How does this remind you of the method you used to determine the perimeter of a rectangle?

What two parts of the rectangle did each set of footprints walk about?

How does the number sentence describe what the footprints do?

What might be an easier way to find the perimeter using what these footprints did?

How many sets of footprints walked the same distance on corresponding sides?

How does the number sentence describe what the footprints do?

What might be an easier way to find the perimeter using what these footprints did?

What is the easiest way for you to remember how to find the perimeter of a rectangle?

Problem Solving: Perimeter Stories

Developing story problems helps students not only to practice solving the problems but to pay attention to the various components necessary to solve them.

Bring a small box into class and a ruler and ask students how they can determine how much string is needed to go around the box. They will respond "measure the sides." As a volunteer measures the length of each side, students can draw quick sketches and record the lengths. If all four sides are measured, most students will add up all four sides. This provides an opportunity to ask if all four sides had to be measured and for students to recognize that only two sides need to be measured.

After solving the situation, ask what information is necessary to solve the problem and clarify that only length and width are needed to find the perimeter of a rectangle. As a class, write a story problem about this situation.

Allowing students time to work in small groups to write a problem on their own about similar situations reinforces their understanding. Trading the problems with another group allows practice and a check for correctness.

After students have developed their own story problems, they are more apt to successfully apply what they have learned to those written by others. Encourage them to use the successful strategies of drawing a sketch and recording measurements on it to help comprehend the situation.

Solutions

1. 24 ft
2. 160 ft
3. 26 blocks
4. 62 ft
5. 96 in
6. 76 in
7. 44 cm
8. 4605 ft
9. 72 in
10. No, the door is only 6.5 ft high.

PERIMETER AND AREA OF RECTANGLES © 2010 AIMS Education Foundation

Perimeter Stories

To solve each problem, draw a sketch of the shape and record the numbers you know.

1. The fence around the garden is a triangle. Each side measures 8 feet. How long is the fence?

2. On your little league baseball team, you run the bases pretty fast. The distance between each base is 40 feet. How far do you run when you hit a home run?

3. The route from home to school is 6 blocks, from school to soccer practice is 8 blocks, from soccer practice to Tommy's is 7 blocks, and then 5 more blocks to home again. What is the round trip distance?

4. The garden at church measures 13 feet wide by 18 feet long. What is its perimeter?

5. The stop sign at the corner measures 12 inches on a side. What is the measure around the octagon?

6. A jigsaw puzzle of elephant seals basking in the sun by the ocean measures 16 inches by 22 inches when completed. What is its perimeter?

7. The largest U.S. currency in circulation is the $100 bill. It measures 15.5 cm long by 6.5 cm wide. What is its perimeter?

8. The Pentagon in Washington D.C. is one of the world's largest office buildings. The complex has 5 sides and 5 floors. The length of each outer wall is 921 feet. How far do you walk going around the Pentagon?

9. In order to frame a picture that measures 13 inches by 23 inches, what length of wood trim will you need?

10. The perimeter of a standard door is 18 feet. If the width is 2.5 feet, will a seven-foot basketball player fit through the door without bending over? Explain.

PERIMETER AND AREA OF RECTANGLES

MEASURING PUZZLE PIECES

How can you measure how much material it takes to cover a puzzle piece?

This activity introduces area as a covering and how the regular shape of a square unit is used to measure covering. Students cover puzzle pieces with area tiles as a unit of measure. By combining the pieces into rectangles, students recognize that area is the sum of the areas of the parts.

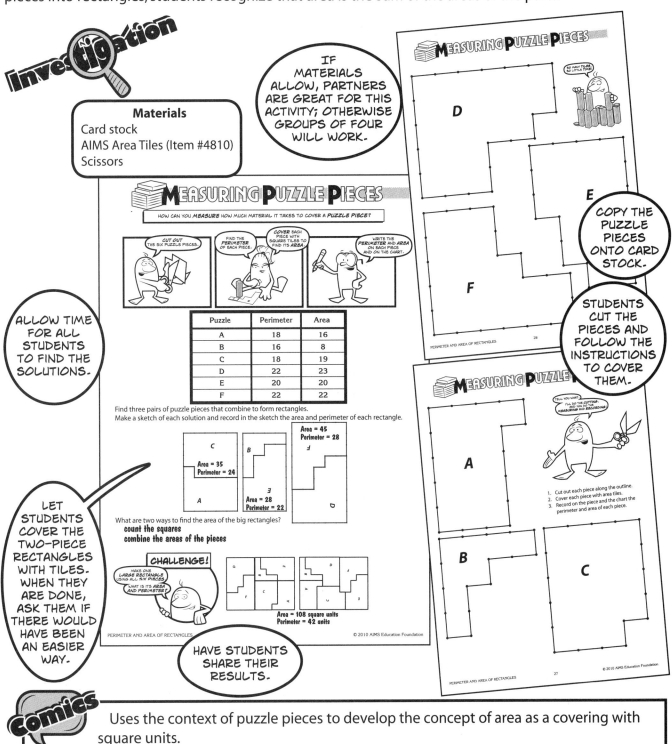

Uses the context of puzzle pieces to develop the concept of area as a covering with square units.

How can you *measure* how much material it takes to cover a *puzzle piece*?

Puzzle	Perimeter	Area
A		
B		
C		
D		
E		
F		

Find three pairs of puzzle pieces that combine to form rectangles.
Make a sketch of each solution and record in the sketch the area and perimeter of each rectangle.

What are two ways to find the area of the big rectangles?

PERIMETER AND AREA OF RECTANGLES

MEASURING PUZZLE PIECES

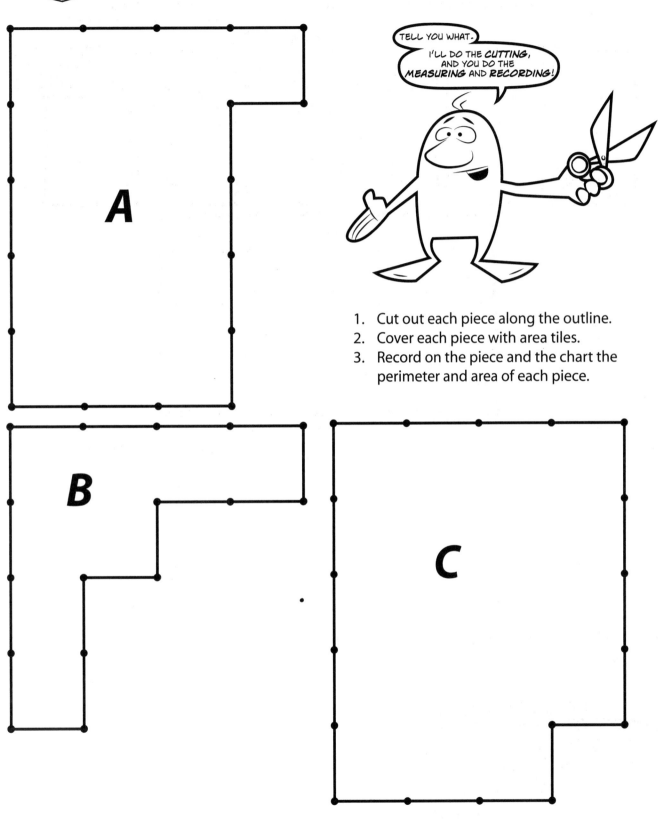

1. Cut out each piece along the outline.
2. Cover each piece with area tiles.
3. Record on the piece and the chart the perimeter and area of each piece.

PERIMETER AND AREA OF RECTANGLES   27   © 2010 AIMS Education Foundation

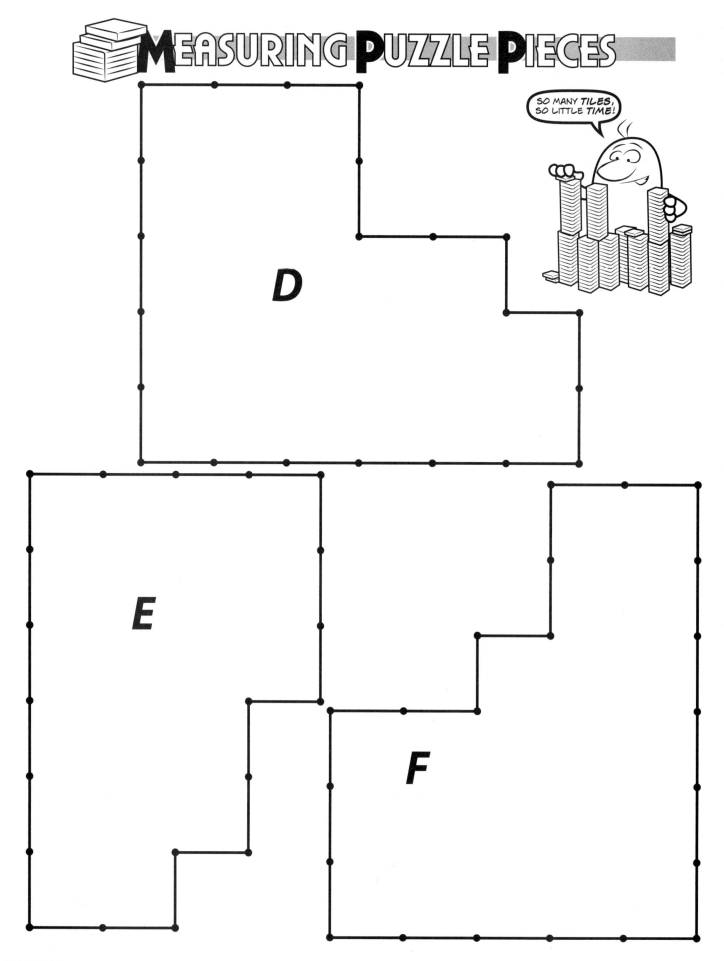

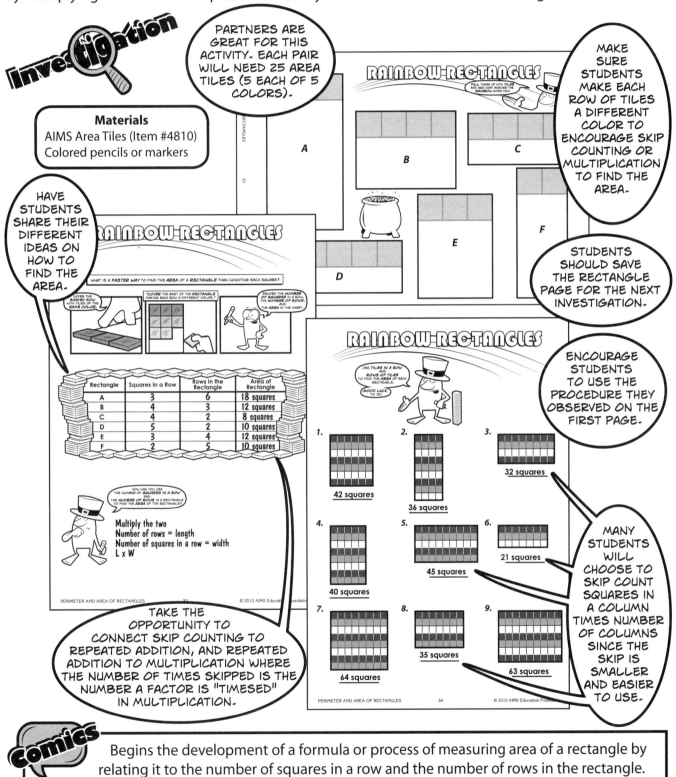

RAINBOW RECTANGLES

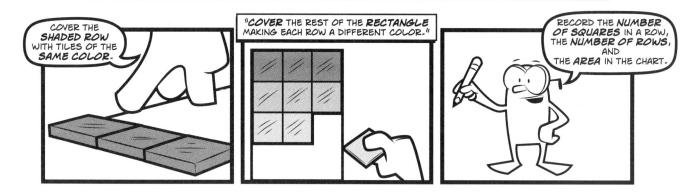

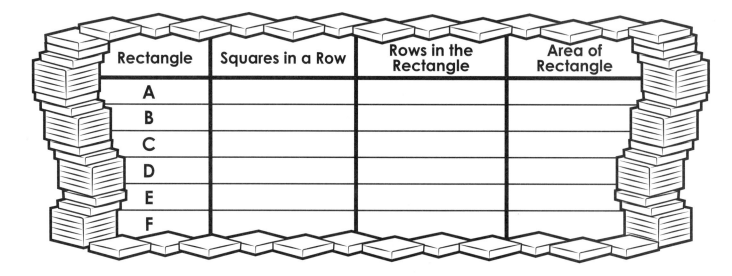

Rectangle	Squares in a Row	Rows in the Rectangle	Area of Rectangle
A			
B			
C			
D			
E			
F			

PERIMETER AND AREA OF RECTANGLES

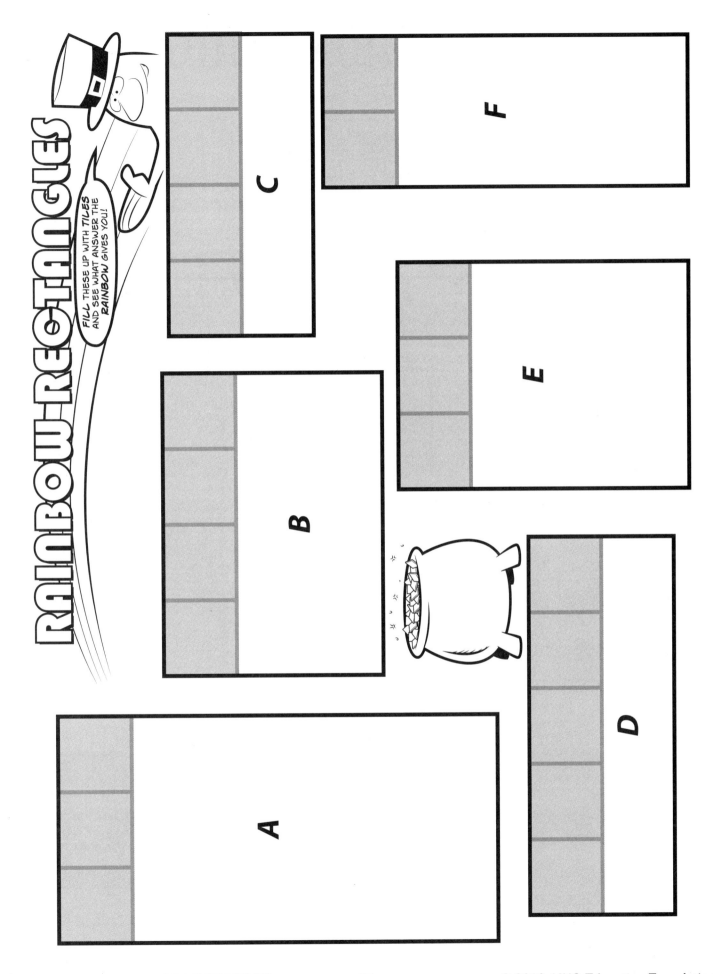

RAINBOW RECTANGLES

USE *TILES IN A ROW* AND *ROWS OF TILES* TO FIND THE *AREA* OF EACH RECTANGLE.

GOOD LUCK TO YE!

1.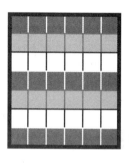

2.

3.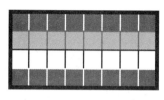

4.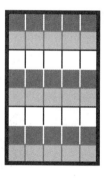

5.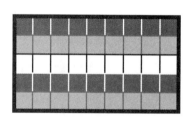

6.

7.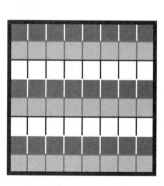

8.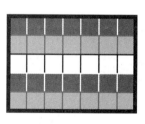

9.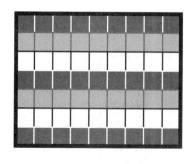

PERIMETER AND AREA OF RECTANGLES

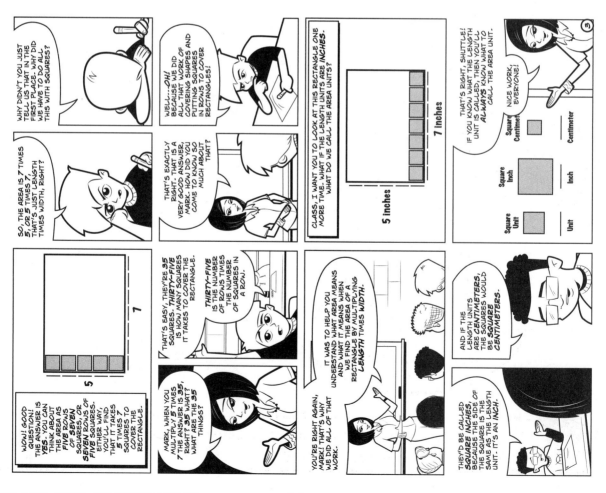

PERIMETER AND AREA OF RECTANGLES

What do you need to know about a rectangle to determine its area?

Area is a measure of covering. Multiplying the number of squares in a row by the number of rows, or length times width, tells how many squares it takes to cover a rectangle.

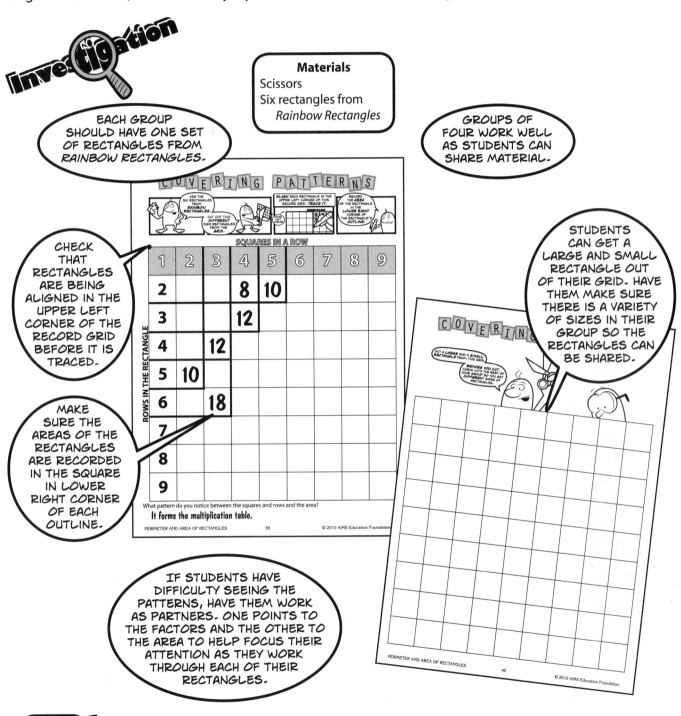

Reinforces the concept of finding area by multiplying the numbers of squares in a row by the number of rows in a rectangle.

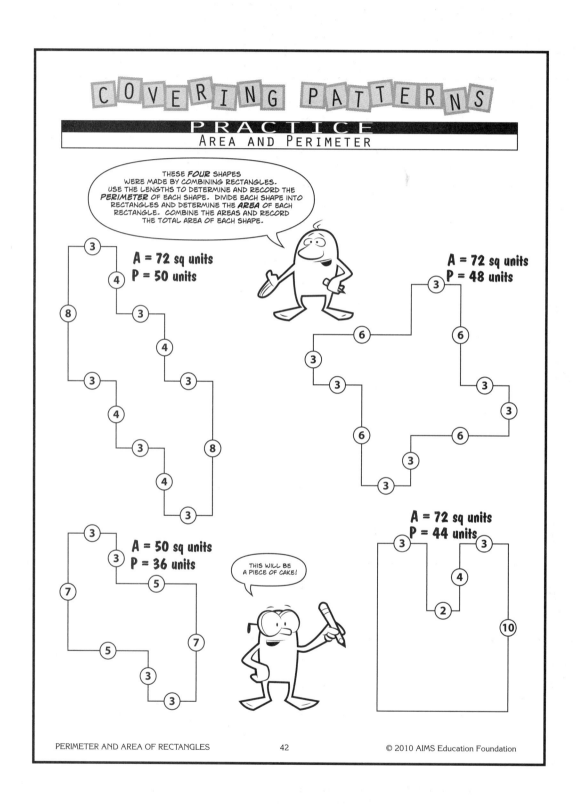

What pattern do you notice between the squares and rows and the area?

PERIMETER AND AREA OF RECTANGLES

COVERING PATTERNS

Cut a LARGE and a SMALL RECTANGLE from this grid.

BEFORE YOU CUT, check with the rest of your group so you get DIFFERENT sizes of rectangles.

PERIMETER AND AREA OF RECTANGLES

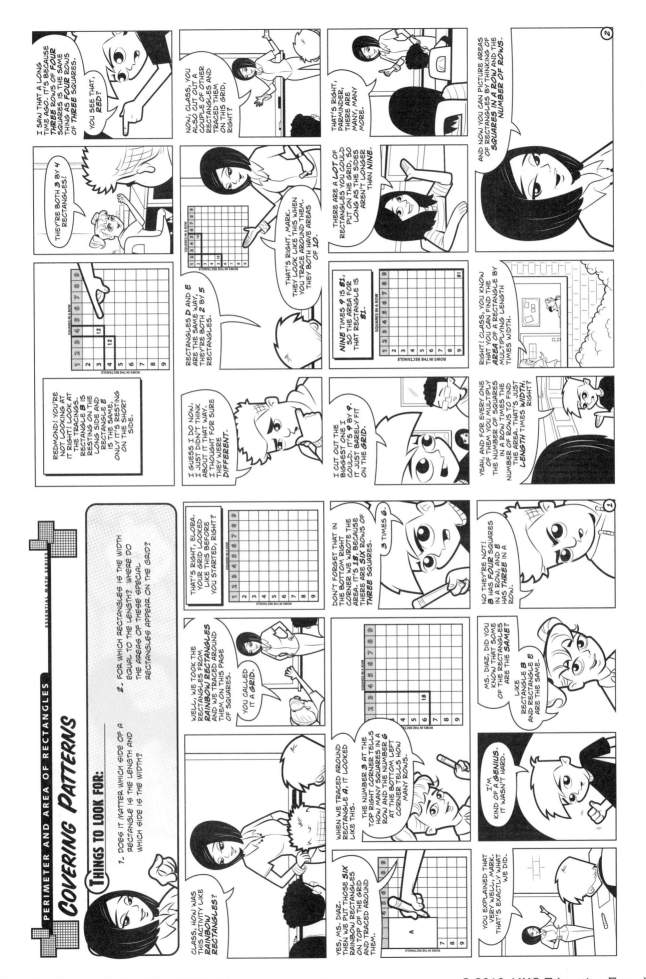

COVERING PATTERNS

PRACTICE
Area and Perimeter

PERIMETER AND AREA OF RECTANGLES

Framing the Facts

How are area measures of rectangles like the multiplication table of facts?

The area model of multiplication is based on the area rectangles. Developing the multiplication table by making rectangles encourages students to understand area as a multiplicative process.

Materials
Scissors

> STUDENTS CAN COMPLETE THE MULTIPLICATION FRAME INDIVIDUALLY BUT CAN WORK COLLABORATIVELY TO CHECK CORRECTNESS.

Framing the Facts

CUT OUT THE FRAMING TOOL ALONG THE WHITE DOTTED LINE AND ALIGN IT TO FORM A DARK FRAME AROUND A **RECTANGLE** OF WHITE SQUARES.

RECORD THE NUMBER OF SQUARES IN A ROW IN THE **UPPER RIGHT SQUARE**, THE NUMBER OF ROWS IN THE **LOWER LEFT SQUARE**, AND THE AREA IN THE **LOWER RIGHT SQUARE** OF THE RECTANGLE.

KEEP MOVING THE **FRAMING TOOL** MAKING RECTANGLES AND RECORDING THE SIZES UNTIL YOU SEE PATTERNS THAT LET YOU **FILL THE GRID**.

How are area measures of rectangles like the multiplication table of facts?

The number of tiles in a row and the number of rows are the factors and the area is the product. The area measures of rectangles forms the multiplication table. Rather than count all of the squares in a rectangle, what would be a short-cut to finding the area?

Multiply the lengths of the sides—L x W

> MOVE AROUND TO SEE THAT THE FRAMING TOOL IS ALIGNED. CHECK TO SEE THAT THE NUMBERS OF SQUARES AND ROWS AND AREAS ARE RECORDED IN THE CORRECT POSITIONS.

> ALLOW STUDENTS TO COMPLETE THE TABLE AS SOON AS THEY RECOGNIZE A PATTERN IN A ROW OR A COLUMN.

> AS STUDENTS FINISH, HAVE THEM DISCUSS THE PATTERNS THEY USED TO FILL IN THE GRID. THEY SHOULD MENTION SKIP COUNTING OR MULTIPLICATION.

> EMPHASIZE THE MULTIPLICATION OF THE LENGTH OF THE SIDES OF A RECTANGLE TO FIND AREA.

RECTANGLE FRAME / **FRAMING TOOL**

1	2	3	4	5	6	7	8	9
2	4	6	8	10	12	14	16	18
3	6	9	12	15	18	21	24	27
4	8	12	16	20	24	28	32	36
5	10	15	20	25	30	35	40	45
6	12	18	24	30	36	42	48	54
7	14	21	28	35	42	49	56	63
8	16	24	32	40	48	56	64	72
9	18	27	36	45	54	63	72	81

The multiplication table is developed dynamically with multiple rectangles. This provides an opportunity to practice area measurement and the multiplication facts.

Develops the relationship between area and the multiplication table to reinforce the concept of area as a multiplicative process.

Framing the Facts

CUT OUT THE *FRAMING TOOL* ALONG THE WHITE DOTTED LINE AND ALIGN IT TO FORM A DARK FRAME AROUND A *RECTANGLE* OF WHITE SQUARES.

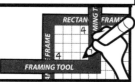

RECORD THE NUMBER OF SQUARES IN A ROW IN THE *UPPER RIGHT SQUARE*, THE NUMBER OF ROWS IN THE *LOWER LEFT SQUARE*, AND THE AREA IN THE *LOWER RIGHT SQUARE* OF THE RECTANGLE.

KEEP MOVING THE *FRAMING TOOL* MAKING RECTANGLES AND RECORDING THE SIZES UNTIL YOU SEE PATTERNS THAT LET YOU *FILL THE GRID*.

How are area measures of rectangles like the multiplication table of facts?

Rather than count all of the squares in a rectangle, what would be a short-cut to finding the area?

RECTANGLE FRAME

(10 × 10 grid)

RECTANGLE FRAME — FRAMING TOOL — FRAMING TOOL

PERIMETER AND AREA OF RECTANGLES

Animation

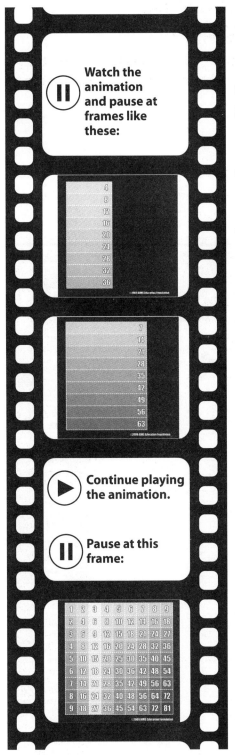

What is the relationship between the areas of rectangles and multiplication?

What dimension is different in each rectangle in a set?

What pattern do you see in the areas of each set of rectangles?

What patterns do you see in the areas aligned in each column?

What patterns do you see in the areas aligned in each row?

Why is the alignment of the areas of these 81 rectangles the same as the multiplication table?

How can knowing the multiplication facts help you find the area of a rectangle?

Problem Solving: Square Thinking About Party Trays

The situation is posed to find a combination of party trays with perimeters of 12, 14, 16, and 18 that will hold 25 square brownies. By forming all the possible trays from perimeter strips and then covering each tray with area tiles that represent brownies, students generate all the solutions. This gives them a great deal of practice in dealing with area as covering, while reinforcing the concept of perimeter as distance around.

Materials
Scissors
Tape
AIMS Area Tiles (Item #4810)

Students working in groups of four should share the work of building rectangles and covering the trays. However, each student should keep a record in order to gain practice in determining the areas of rectangles.

Get the class started on construction by modeling the process of forming the tray. Tape two perimeter strips together, and tape them into a loop. Crease four corners to make the loop into a rectangular region. Cover the interior of the rectangular region with area tiles and sketch the results. Then change the fold on two opposite angles to form a different sized rectangular region. If changing the size of the rectangle is too difficult for students, give the group more perimeter strips and let them make multiple rectangles of the same perimeter.

After completing the investigation, discuss the patterns that arose. Students may recognize that as one side increased by a unit, the adjacent side decreased by a unit. This leads to the recognition that the sum of the two dimensions is half the perimeter. For area, students may recognize that the region with the greatest area is closest to a square.

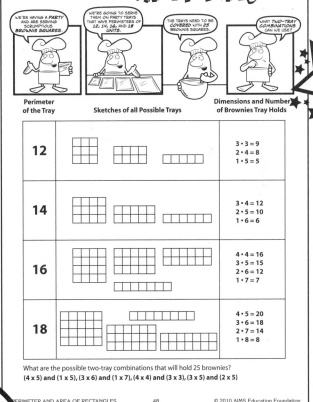

Covers the problem-solving process that might arise when dealing with an application of area and perimeter in a problem-solving situation.

SQUARE THINKING ABOUT PARTY TRAYS

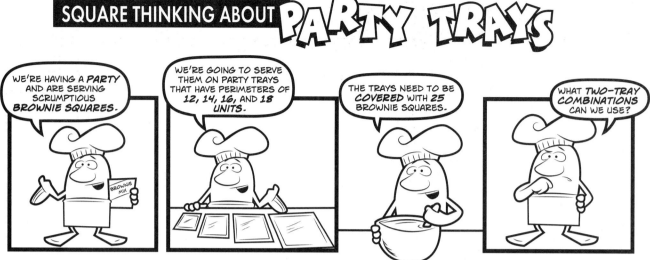

Perimeter of the Tray — **Sketches of all Possible Trays** — **Dimensions and Number of Brownies Tray Holds**

Perimeter	Sketches of all Possible Trays	Dimensions and Number of Brownies Tray Holds
12		
14		
16		
18		

What are the possible two-tray combinations that will hold 25 brownies?

PERIMETER AND AREA OF RECTANGLES

Perimeter and Area of Rectangles Assessment

In both assessments students are confronted with a situation that requires a decision on how to design a play area.

Fencing the Play Area

In the first assessment, a play area is to be surrounded by 18 sections of fence. The perimeter is kept constant, but the area changes. Four rectangles can be formed that have a perimeter of 18 units of length, but each has a different area. Providing each student with an area tile, helps him or her to mark out the perimeter as was done in *Side Line Counts*. Students will find it easier if they recognize the pattern that as the length decreases by one, the width increases by one. Students may begin to recognize that the closer to a square a rectangle becomes, the more area it has for the same perimeter.

Solutions

Rectangle Dimensions (sections)	Area (sq. sections)
1 x 8	8
2 x 7	14
3 x 6	18
4 x 5	20

Build the 4 x 5 rectangle; it has the greatest play area.

Laying Play Area Mats

In the second assessment, a play area is to be covered with 24 square foam tiles. The area is kept constant, but the perimeter changes. Four rectangles can be formed that have an area of 24 squares, but each has a different perimeter. Providing each student with 24 area tiles helps him or her make the different possible arrangements. Students will find it easier if they recognize the pattern that the possible dimensions are factors of 24. This allows you to assess how well they have internalized the idea of area as a multiplicative process. Students may begin to recognize that the closer to a square a rectangle becomes, the less perimeter it has for the same area.

Solutions

Play Area Dimensions (sections)	Fence Needed (sections)
1 x 24	50
2 x 12	28
3 x 8	22
4 x 6	20

Build the 4 x 6 area; it needs the least fencing.

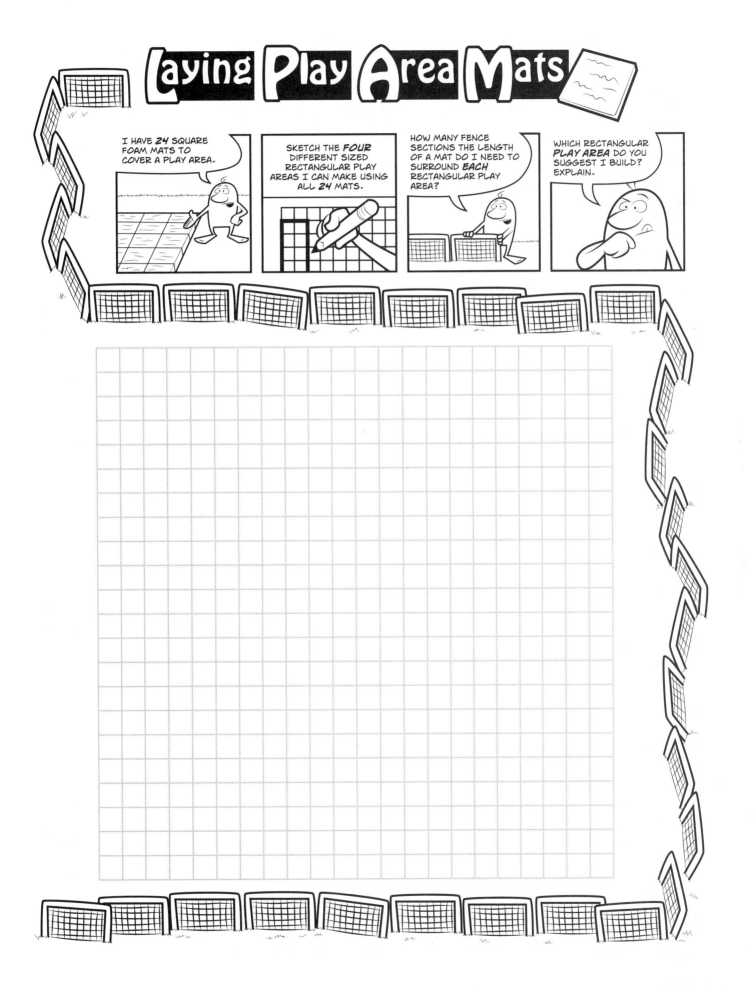

GLOSSARY

THIS PAGE IS GOOD FOR REFERENCE

THERE'S A LOT OF GOOD INFO DOWN THERE!

MEASUREMENTS

Perimeter of a rectangle is the distance around. It is the sum of the lengths of the four sides.

Area is a measure of covering. The units are squares—square centimeters, square inches, or, in general, square units. The area of a rectangle is the number of squares (square units) needed to cover the inside (interior) of the rectangle.

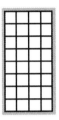

$A = L \times W$

The **formula** for the area of a rectangle is length times width. What that means is that the number of squares needed to cover the interior of the rectangle is the number of squares in a row times the number of rows. The length can tell you how many squares are in a row and then the width tells you how many rows.

ATTRIBUTES

A **rectangle** is a four-sided two-dimensional shape, where the sides are line segments.

Each corner point is called a **vertex.**

Two sides of a rectangle meet at each vertex or corner point to form a right angle. Saying that a rectangle has four right angles is the more mathematical way of saying it has four square corners.

Opposite sides of a rectangle are the same length, and they are parallel. Opposite sides are two sides that are across from each other.

PERIMETER AND AREA OF RECTANGLES

Standards from Guiding Documents

Project 2061 Benchmark

- *Length can be thought of as unit lengths joined together, area as a collection of unit squares, and volume as a set of unit cubes.*
- *Areas of irregular shapes can be found by dividing them into squares and triangles.*

American Association for the Advancement of Science
Benchmarks for Science Literacy
Oxford University Press. New York. 1993.

NCTM Standards 2000*

- *Understand, select, and use units of appropriate size and type to measure angles, perimeter, area, surface area, and volume*
- *Use geometric models to solve problems in other areas of mathematics, such as number and measurement*
- *Develop, understand, and use formulas to find the area of rectangles and related triangles and parallelograms*
- *Develop strategies for estimating the perimeters, areas, and volumes of irregular shapes*

Reprinted with permission from
Principles and Standards for School Mathematics 2000
by the National Council of Teachers of Mathematics
All rights reserved.

Unit Materials List

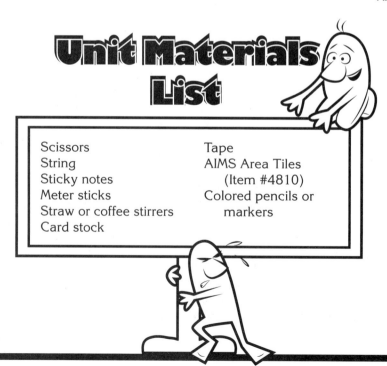

Scissors
String
Sticky notes
Meter sticks
Straw or coffee stirrers
Card stock

Tape
AIMS Area Tiles
  (Item #4810)
Colored pencils or
  markers

The Story of Perimeter and Area of Rectangles

The focus of this unit is on perimeter and area of rectangles. The unit begins with the concepts in general, and then applies them to rectangles, and finally generalizes the formulas for perimeter and area of rectangles.

Prior Learning

In earlier grades, students learned that a rectangle has four sides, that opposite sides have equal lengths, and all of the angles are right angles. They will probably also know that opposite sides of a rectangle are parallel, and that a rectangle is really a special kind of parallelogram. Students may or may not have thought about the fact that a rectangle surrounds a region of the plane. We call this the interior or the inside of the rectangle. While students have learned these things about rectangles in an earlier grade, it will be important to review these attributes.

Measuring Rectangles

This unit is really about measuring rectangles. There are three different measurements that we use to measure different attributes of a rectangle. The first is **length measure.** We can measure the lengths of the sides, the lengths of the diagonals, and the perimeter of a rectangle.

The second kind of measurement is **area measure** of a rectangle. This is a measurement of the interior of the rectangle. It is a measurement of the region that is surrounded or bounded by the rectangle.

Finally, there is **angle measure.** While students will not actually be measuring angles in this unit, it will be important for them to understand that each of the angles of a rectangle is a right angle, and that this is one of the distinguishing characteristics of a rectangle.

Concept of Perimeter

Perimeter is a length measurement. Perimeter is simply the distance around a shape. While we may find the perimeter of a shape like a triangle, parallelogram, or rectangle by measuring each of the sides and adding them up, we can also find it by wrapping a string around the shape and then measuring the length of the string.

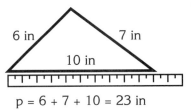

p = 6 + 7 + 10 = 23 in

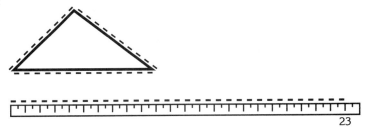

Concept of Area

Area is a measure of covering. Area is a measurement of the interior of a two-dimensional shape. The units used to measure area are always square units that correspond with the length units. In other words, if the length unit is an inch, then the area unit will be a square with a side of one inch. The way to directly measure the area of such a region is by completely covering it with units and counting.

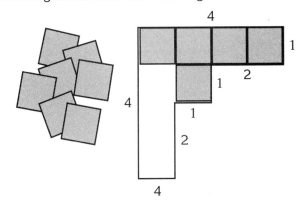

PERIMETER AND AREA OF RECTANGLES © 2010 AIMS Education Foundation

Perimeter of Rectangles

Perimeter is a length measure: the sum of the lengths of the sides. One of the things we know about rectangles is that opposite sides have the same length. That means that to find the length of all four sides of a rectangle, we need only make two measurements: length and width. The sum of the length and width gives us one half of the perimeter. If we multiply by two, we have the perimeter. Or, we could simply add twice the length plus twice the width. Of course, any one of these ways will give us the perimeter of the rectangle.

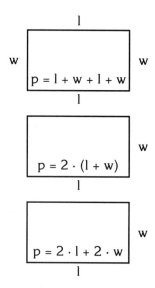

Area of Rectangles

Measuring the area of a rectangle using square units is especially easy because of the rectangle's right angles. While squares can be laid out to cover the rectangle and then counted to find the area, a more efficient way would be to think of laying out the squares in rows and noting the number of rows needed to cover the interior of the rectangle. Multiplying the number of squares in a row times the number of rows is then a more efficient way to count the number of squares.

By further noticing that the length of the rectangle corresponds to the number of squares in a row, and the number of rows corresponds to the width, we then have made meaningful the formula, A = l x w, for finding the area of a rectangle.

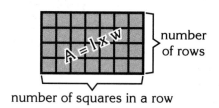

Area of Rectangles and Multiplication Facts

Students completing this unit know their multiplication facts; however, they may not make the connection between those facts and finding the areas of rectangles. By superimposing rectangles over a multiplication table, students can see the number of squares in a row across the top and the number of rows down the left side. The area can be read in the lower right corner. Moreover, every rectangle that is not a square can be positioned on the grid in two different ways. A five by three rectangle can be viewed as having five squares in a row and three rows, or it might have three squares in a row and five rows. It is the same rectangle, the area turns out to be the same either way—an illustration of the commutative property of multiplication.

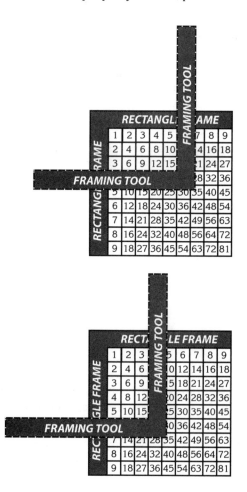

Summary

The unit starts with the ideas of perimeter as the distance around a shape, and area as the measure of covering. These measures are then applied to rectangles, which is the focus of the unit. The unit ends with an activity that makes a connection between using length times width to find the areas of rectangles and the meaning of multiplication.

Using Comics to Teach Math

The *Essential Math* units contain comics. They generally are used to clarify and review the class investigation.

Rationale
Comics were chosen for several reasons. First, students are very comfortable with the comic format and are much more motivated to read the material because of the medium. Secondly, it has been found that material that is written in comic format is more easily understood than when the same information is delivered in narrative format. This may be true for several reasons:
- Comics combine images and words to help students make sense of the concepts and relationships that are the focus of an activity.
- Comics are more casual so academic vocabulary can be understood through visual clues and common language.
- Comics by nature deliver the same information with fewer words. As a result, the author must be brief and clear and must craft the dialogue carefully.
- Comics are naturally sequential. Each frame is a snapshot. This provides a progressive development of ideas with a chance for the reader to stop at each point to comprehend what is being said.
- The visual nature of the comics allows them to reinforce the conceptual understanding introduced in the investigation. The affective and cognitive benefits of comics make them an excellent resource for reading in the content area of math.

Possible Usage
Directed Reading: The comics may be distributed to be read individually either at school or home. Direct the students to do pre-reading by reading the summary questions and scanning the comic. When students have completed the reading, have a class discussion on the summary questions.

Reader's Theater: Assign students different characters in the comic and have them do an oral presentation. If time allows, split the class into teams to practice reading the script and then give multiple performances, or assign each group a page to read. Engage more students by providing word cards of key words. Have non-reading students hold up the cards whenever their word is said. Be sure to have a discussion after reading the comic that includes the summary questions.

Teaching Scripts: While time constraints may prevent the use of the comics with students, the teacher can glean the finer points of the concepts and teaching strategies from them. The comic provides a script of how this might be presented to the class and how a discussion might be encouraged.

Formats
The comics can be copied for the students or displayed on a computer or projector. The paper copies can be made from the book or pdf files on the compact disc. The pdf files come in a full-page version or the more efficient two-page version found in the book. For viewing with a computer, there is a full-page view. When using a projector, choose the slide show version with large easily read frames.

Using Animations to Teach Math

Each *Essential Math* unit contains animations that provide culminating experiences for big ideas. As a visual medium, animations provide a very powerful tool for understanding and memory. If a picture is worth a thousand words, an animation is worth many times more.

The Dynamic Nature of an animation allows the viewer to make connections and build relationships not available with a static picture. As the animation runs, the student should be asked to identify what actions they see happening, the relationships within those events, and how the animation relates to prior experiences in the unit.

A Usage Guide is provided for each animation as a student record page. It can be used as a guide for class discussion. It may be used as a record sheet for students or may be used by the teachers as a guide for when to pause the animation and elicit class discussion.

The animations are available on the compact disc and need to be played through a computer. The player allows for pausing and frame-by-frame movement. They are best viewed by a class using a projector, but may be displayed on a single monitor.

MODEL OF LEARNING
Math and Science

The Model of Learning is a foundational component of AIMS lessons. It consists of four environments in which we learn about our world. These environments are represented by four geometric figures: a circle, a triangle, a square, and a hexagon.

An AIMS lesson will start with a *Key Question*. It is this question that leads students into an encounter with the four environments of learning.

For example, the Key Question for an activity might be: "How does the length of a piece of rope change if you tie knots in it?"

The circle corresponds to the real world. It involves *doing* something with or to concrete objects. This environment emphasizes the use of sensory input, involving *observing, touching (taking apart/putting together), smelling, hearing, tasting*. Observations here can be qualitative or quantitative (counting and measuring). The use of multiple senses causes activity in the parts of the brain where that type of information is processed, thus establishing or reinforcing mental connectors.

The activity would begin in the circle with students tying knots one by one in a piece of rope and measuring the length of the rope each time another knot is tied.

The triangle represents the abstractions of *reading* and *writing*. It is the real world symbolized in words and numbers. Meaning is attached to these abstractions because of what was done in the circle. This environment consists of recording numbers that result from the counting and measuring. It may involve writing a description of what was observed. Reading the rubber band books or comics found in the AIMS materials are included in this environment. Students work here when they read their textbooks or do the computation exercises.

In the knot-tying example, the students would next move to the triangle where the number of knots and the length of the rope are recorded in a table.

The square represents *picturing* or *illustrating* the real world. Graphs, diagrams, drawings, or an isometric drawing are examples of the pictures that can be used. The square might simply involve picturing what was recorded in the triangle. It could also be an illustration of an object or event that occurred while students were working in the circle environment. Both of these situations are constructed from student input; however, the drawing or graph or other illustration could be one that is imposed upon a student for interpretation purposes.

Relating to the example of tying knots, the student might move from the triangle to the square to construct a graph of the relationship between the number of knots in the rope and the length of the rope. Or the student could have moved directly from the circle to the square to construct the graph.

Finally, the hexagon represents *thinking, analyzing, generalizing, creating formulas, hypothesizing,* and *applying*. What did we find out? What does it mean? Is there a relationship? What is it? Is there a formula? To what other situations might this apply?

Students in the example might look back at the table and be asked, "By how much does the length of the rope change each time another knot is tied? How does this show up in the graph?" Students might note that the graph is a line. "What is the slope of the line? How does the slope show up in the table? What would be the length if there were 10 knots in the rope? How about if there were n knots in the rope? How could you find the length without measuring? Could you write this as an equation?"

The arrows pointing to and away from each of the environments suggest the importance of moving back and forth between the environments. To generalize the relationship between the number of knots and the length of the rope required going back and forth between the hexagon, the square, and the triangle. Once the formula is found, it can be applied to another situation that might be posed in the circle.

Perhaps the most important thing the Model of Learning does is to remind us of the four learning environments and help us think about how to structure an activity or lesson so that students are constructing and reinforcing the concepts and relationships. This is accomplished by moving back and forth between these environments. The triangle is where students too often spend most of their time in school activities. While this environment is not unimportant, the other environments give students something other than the tip of their pencil with which to think. AIMS activities are designed around these environments and make moving back and forth between these environments natural and meaningful.